THE DEATH OF COOL

THE DEATH OF COOL

by Alan Pollock

WARNER/CHAPPELL PLAYS

LONDON

A Warner Music Group Company

THE DEATH OF COOL
First published in 1999
by Warner/Chappell Plays Ltd
Griffin House, 161 Hammersmith Road, London W6 8BS

ISBN 0 85676 234 2

To Simon, with thanks

THE DEATH OF COOL was first performed at the Hampstead Theatre (Jenny Topper, Artistic Director) on 20th May, 1999. The cast was as follows:

SWITCH	Colin Tierney
RICHIE	Gideon Turner
LISA	Susannah Doyle
TARA	Georgia Mackenzie
WAITER/ SAVAGE/ NURSE	Colin Haigh
NEWMAN	Jem Wall

Directed by Gemma Bodinetz
Designed by Es Devlin
Lighting design by John Titcombe
Sound by Fergus O'Hare for Aura Sound

The action takes place in various locations in north London in the present.

ACT ONE

Scene One

*The living room of a North London flat. The overall
impression is of cultured hedonism – mountains of records,
CDs and videos together with the equipment – palpably
expensive – necessary for playing them.*

*On one wall there is an enormous reproduction film poster –
Chet Baker in* Let's Get Lost. *In another area a kind of mini
recording studio – with record decks, amps, a keyboard,
computer and mixing desk.*

*The room is dominated by two items of furniture – an
enormous, comfortable looking sofa and a large coffee table
covered with ashtrays, books, magazines and empty drinks
cans. Also a pair of scales.*

*The one curious and unexpected feature of the room – above
the fireplace – is a kind of impromptu shrine. A blown-up
passport photo of a thirty-something man surrounded by
coloured lights on a green wire – a kitsch and ironic
religious statement of some kind.*

It is early evening.

SWITCH – *twenty-nine, ugly-beautiful – stands in front of the
sofa. He wears a dirty raincoat with Jarvis Cocker glasses.*
RICHIE – *twenty-three, insolently good-looking – watches him.*
RICHIE *has just come in, and there are labelled shopping bags
on the sofa beside him.*

SWITCH   (*a performance*) Babylon the Great is fallen,
                and is become the habitation of devils. For all
                nations have drunk of the wrath of her
                fornication, and the kings of the earth have
                committed fornication with her, and the
                merchants of the earth are waxed rich through
                the abundance of her delicacies . . .

RICHIE   Go on.

SWITCH   But the fearful, and the unbelieving, and the
          abominable, and the murderers, and the
          whoremongerers, and the sorcerers . . . they
          shall have their part in the lake which burneth
          with fire and brimstone. (*Beat.*) You think
          with the drool or without?

RICHIE   Try it without.

SWITCH   But the fearful, and the unbelieving . . . and
          the estate agents, and the lawyers . . . they
          shall have their part in the lake which burneth
          with fire and brimstone.

RICHIE   The thing I always notice about these guys . . .
          they've always got cuts on their hands.

SWITCH   Cuts.

RICHIE   And plasters. Like in weird places.

SWITCH   I can do cuts. And plasters. (*Beat.*) But what
          about the script? You think it's too obvious? I
          figure at least with the God stuff people know
          where they are. There's like a long and
          honourable tradition. Whereas the other stuff
          – you know – vampires stole my lunch money,
          blah blah blah blah blah . . . it's too kitsch . . .
          it's too tabloid . . .

RICHIE   I don't know.

SWITCH   What do you think?

          (*Beat.*)

RICHIE   What do I think? I think: Don't rock the boat.
          That's what I think.

SWITCH   You don't understand. Something like this.
          You gotta keep moving. You gotta stay ahead.

RICHIE   What happens if they suss? Just call in the
          goons?

SWITCH   The goons?

RICHIE   Slap you in a jacket, throw away the key?

SWITCH   It's not gonna happen.

RICHIE   Why not?

SWITCH   Because they're too stupid. And because it's
            too much trouble. All they want is me out of
            the office . . .

RICHIE   You reckon?

SWITCH   And the quickest way to achieve that is to
            send me to the loony doctor. Then the easiest
            thing for *him* is to give me the drugs and the
            sick note.

RICHIE   If you say so.

SWITCH   It's simple. (*A visionary gleam.*) This whole
            thing's like some . . . bureaucratic martial art.

RICHIE   Yeah?

SWITCH   Use your opponent's weight. Use your
            opponent's inertia. (*Beat.*) All *they* want is an
            easy life. All *you* want is the money.

RICHIE   (*getting up*) The Bruce Lee of benefit fraud.

SWITCH   Exactly. What's in the bag?

RICHIE   (*going to place the record on the turntable*) I
            went to this place. In the market. They got all
            these white labels and acetates. Stuff no one
            else's got . . .

SWITCH   What did you get?

RICHIE   I said I wanted something . . . you know . . .
                extreme . . . like a total headfuck. Some noise
                no one ever heard before . . .

SWITCH   What did they give you?

RICHIE   This.

                (RICHIE *activates the deck. A blast of abrasive,
                dysfunctional noise. Lets it play for a second
                before turning it down.*)

                It's from Finland. They got like this club.
                Inside the Arctic Circle. They have this big
                party, every June. Everyone stays up for a
                month, then afterwards, the ones that aren't,
                like, dead – or completely insane – they go
                into the studio and make records . . .

SWITCH   I thought the idea was *elation*. Lift people up.
                Make them feel like they're having a good
                time . . .

RICHIE   You think I should stick to the tunes?

SWITCH   Up to you. Give people what they want and
                they end up despising you. Make it clear you
                despise *them* and they can't help loving
                you . . .

RICHIE   The oracle speaks.

                (RICHIE *takes off the record, starts to put it
                away.*)

SWITCH   Where's the spot?

RICHIE   It's just a bar. Down near Old Street. But it's
                like a showcase. Loads of agents and club
                reps.

SWITCH   Tonight?

RICHIE   Tomorrow.

SWITCH   What are you doing tonight?

RICHIE   I said I'd meet someone. Sort of check out the
              venue for tomorrow.

              (*Beat.* RICHIE *picks up a towel from the back
              of an armchair, as if about to go for a bath.*)

              What about you?

SWITCH   No plans really. There's this classic Hancock
              on satellite. The one where him and Sid each
              think the other one's trying to kill them.

RICHIE   Right. Listen, Switch. You couldn't sort us
              some readies, could you? I'm a little bit short.

SWITCH   How much?

RICHIE   Fifteen? Twenty? Whatever you've got.

              (SWITCH *pulls out an enormous roll from his
              pocket. Peels off a couple of tens.* RICHIE *takes
              them.*)

              You're a star. Mind if I have a bath?

SWITCH   Go for it.

              (*Exit* RICHIE. SWITCH *at a loose end. The phone
              rings. He does not answer. The BT message
              kicks in. Then the voice of a woman.*)

WOMAN'S   Steve? Are you there? Pick up . . . pick up . . .
VOICE
              (*Suddenly animated,* SWITCH *hurries to the
              phone.*)

SWITCH   Yep. Jesus. How are you? *Where* are you?
              (*Long pause.*) *Sure.* Of course. (*He looks
              around the room*). No that's fine. I'm just a
              little . . . you know . . . Look, what time?
              (*Beat.*) OK. I'll see you tomorrow.

(SWITCH *is palpably thrown by the call. Lights fade.*)

Scene Two

The living room. Around ten-thirty the following night.

SWITCH *sits at one end of the sofa, preparing a coke can for the smoking of freebase cocaine. At the other end of the sofa sits* LISA – *late twenties, pale and washed out, strikingly attractive. Downstage stands* RICHIE – *ironing a pair of expensive, labelled trousers, captivated by* LISA.

LISA	So what is it? This indefinable quality?
SWITCH	I dunno. Just this kind of 'fuck you, I don't care who you are, these are the rules, I made them up' kind of thing.
LISA	So Brando.
SWITCH	Of course.
LISA	Even though he's some doped-out old bastard with a kid that killed someone.
SWITCH	Nobody said they had to have cool kids.
LISA	Maybe that's why.
SWITCH	Why what?
LISA	I mean what the fuck chance've you got? With *Brando* for a father. What's the matter with Dad? I dunno, he decided to stop talking, just kind of mumbles . . . you think he's gonna grow up normal, go to law school?
SWITCH	Actually he did.
RICHIE	Did what?

SWITCH   Go to law school. Or something.

                (*He offers the Coke can – first to* LISA, *who
                declines, then to* RICHIE, *who accepts.*)

                It's like Roger Moore . . .

RICHIE   (*a noticeably poor Roger Moore imitation*)
                Sorry darling – something just came up –

                (*The crack catches his throat. He is racked by
                a coughing fit.*)

SWITCH   Exactly. James Bond *to the life*. But naff.
                Totally un-cool. (*Beat. To* LISA.) I mean who
                would you rather . . . shimmying up the
                drainpipe, dagger between the teeth, skin still
                moist with Adriatic foam . . .

LISA   (*sighs, obviously*) Who do you think?

SWITCH   Precisely. A bald, incomprehensible, milk-
                hefting prole from Edinburgh. Who'd be
                chased off the playing fields of Eton if he so
                much as set foot on them. (*Beat.*) It's
                something intuitive. You've either got it or
                you haven't.

                (*Pause.*)

RICHIE   What's wrong with Roger Moore?

                (*Stage silence – The Man Who Thought Roger
                Moore Was A Better James Bond Than Sean
                Connery . . .*)

SWITCH   What's wrong with Roger Moore? Richie I
                worry about you. I really do.

                (RICHIE *gives him the finger.*)

                (*to* LISA) It's like tonight . . .

LISA   What?

SWITCH   (*to* LISA) He comes back from town, right –
            and he's carrying this thing. He's carrying
            this thing like it's the most precious – the
            most *delicate* thing in the world. I think what
            can it be? A wounded animal? An Art Deco
            vase?

LISA   What was it?

SWITCH   A pair of trousers. This pair of trousers. This
            priceless pair of retro strides you see before
            you . . .

            (RICHIE *has finished.*)

RICHIE   Fuck off.

SWITCH   I keep telling him. Fashion is temporary.
            Class is permanent.

RICHIE   Yeah, well, if I looked like you, I wouldn't get
            in, would I? Never mind get to DJ.

            (SWITCH *takes an enormous hit.* RICHIE
            struggles into the trousers.)

            He's got like this *sitcom* thing . . .

LISA   Sitcom?

RICHIE   It's like Tony and Sid, Fletcher and Godber.
            (*Beat.*) Like he's some *old lag*, dishing it out
            from on high . . .

SWITCH   (*inhaling deeply*) You wanna try some of this.

            (RICHIE *and* LISA *both decline.* SWITCH *is lost
            to the world.*)

LISA   Just ignore him.

RICHIE   He's six foot four, he has size fourteen shoes,
            and his name is Stephen O'Flaherty Waller.
            How do you ignore a thing like that?

LISA   (*getting up*) Try it. Actually what I need is
water . . .

RICHIE   The thing I don't understand is, how come he
never said.

(*She checks.*)

LISA   Why would he?

RICHIE   Lisa Fox. Of the Blue Roses.

LISA   We're not exactly The Manic Street Preachers,
are we? (*Noticing the shrine above the
fireplace.*) What's this?

RICHIE   What? (*Beat.*) Oh, that.

(*At this point the front door bell rings, off.
SWITCH is instantly alert. Exits to answer front
door.*)

Switch calls it The Shrine to The Unknown
Claimant . . .

LISA   But who is it?

RICHIE   The guy who lived here before. Left some
photos and a dole card. Terry Somebody?

(*LISA exits in search of water. Enter TARA –
late twenties, bourgeoise, over-dressed for her
talents – accompanied by SWITCH.*)

SWITCH   Why aren't you in the pub?

TARA   Look, it wasn't my fault.

SWITCH   What do you mean?

TARA   The place was full of hen parties. All these
office girlies with big hair and too much
make-up.

SWITCH	How long did you stay?
TARA	Absolutely ages . . .
SWITCH	You've got to give it a chance . . .
TARA	I *did*. There was too much competition, that's all. And I felt a fool. On my own in a place like that. These ghastly women giving me the eye.
SWITCH	You need to find a corner. Somewhere near the Gents. Catch them on the way out.
TARA	I did.
SWITCH	It's only a matter of time. 'Anyone sitting here?' No, feel free. 'What do you do?' I'm a palmist. I read palms . . .
TARA	I know. (*Beat.*) Look, tell me again . . .
SWITCH	Tell you what?
TARA	It's just the start. I have trouble getting started . . .
	(SWITCH *sighs*.)
SWITCH	All you need is a few details . . .
TARA	This is where I go wrong . . .
SWITCH	Date of birth, place of birth, parents' names, mother's maiden name. Just to help you build up a picture. You tell them last year was a bitch, last year was a low point, but *this* year . . .
TARA	Things are going to pick up . . .

SWITCH	Ask them about their travel plans, if they're going abroad. All I need to know is they're *not* gonna be applying for a passport . . .

(*Re-enter* LISA. *Stops short.*)

SWITCH	Lisa, this is Tara. Tara, Lisa.
LISA	Hi.
TARA	Oh. Hi.

(*Beat.*)

Have we met?

LISA	I don't think so . . .
SWITCH	Lisa and I were at college.

(*Beat.*)

TARA	Wait a moment. Lisa. Lisa Fox. From that band . . . . (*Beat.*) I thought you were on tour. Didn't I see that? You were on this programme. In the middle of the night. With that Danny guy . . .

(*Beat.* LISA *seems to stiffen.*)

SWITCH	Tara acts. She's an actress.
LISA	That's great.
TARA	Yeah. (*Beat.*) Listen . . . am I interrupting something?
LISA	Not at all. In fact, Switch . . . I think I might crash out. No offence, Tara. It's just . . . you guys carry on. Don't let me put a stop to the party . . .

(TARA *sums up the situation.*)

TARA	I can't stay anyway. I was just on my way home . . .
LISA	It's good to meet you . . .
TARA	And you . . .
RICHIE	I'll walk you to the tube.
TARA	What?
RICHIE	I'm on my way out. I'll walk you to the tube.
TARA	Right.
SWITCH	I'll call you, OK? Sometime tomorrow . . .
TARA	Whatever.
RICHIE	(*picking up bulging record bags*) Hey, Switch . . .
SWITCH	What?
RICHIE	I forgot to tell you . . .
SWITCH	Tell me what?
RICHIE	This guy phoned up. Wanted to speak to Stephen.
SWITCH	What guy?
RICHIE	I don't know. Some guy . . .
SWITCH	He called me Stephen?
RICHIE	I told him wrong number, you didn't live here any more . . .
SWITCH	(*concerned*) Well, which?

(*Beat.*)

RICHIE   You didn't live here any more . . . .

SWITCH   (*an edge*) Always stick to the same lie, OK?

RICHIE   *OK.* I'm sorry.

SWITCH   Forget it.

              (*Beat.*)

RICHIE   And your mum called. Says she's seen some
              more jobs, she's sending you the adverts.

SWITCH   What this time?

RICHIE   She didn't say.

SWITCH   Assistant Turkey Inseminator. Imminent start.
              Good prospects.

              (*Beat.*)

RICHIE   Look, I'll see you later, alright?

SWITCH   Knock 'em dead.

RICHIE   Yeah. Right.

              (RICHIE *casts a last glance at* SWITCH *before he
              goes, accompanied by* TARA.)

LISA   What was all that about?

SWITCH   Parents are independent film-makers. They
              moved so he could go to some trendy
              comprehensive. Result? He knows absolutely
              nothing. But he expects the world . . .

LISA   Steve?

SWITCH   What happened to your nails?

LISA   It's a long story.

SWITCH	Are you clean?
LISA	Why do you think I'm biting my nails? (*Beat.*) Who's this? The guy in the photo?
SWITCH	Lisa . . .
LISA	I just need some time. OK?
	(*Beat.*)
SWITCH	Sure. Whatever. (*Beat.*) Stay as long as you like.
	(*She approaches, kisses him on the cheek.*)
LISA	I'm fucked.
SWITCH	Use my room.
LISA	Sure?
SWITCH	I'll sleep in here.
LISA	You're a hero.
	(*She gives him another quick peck, then goes. Lights fade.*)

Scene Three

Next morning. The living room. RICHIE *and* LISA *on the sofa.*

RICHIE	There's a moment. Every evening. It's like it's time. You just need to find the right switch. The right sound. Hit the G-spot, send them wild . . .
LISA	You make it sound like . . .
RICHIE	Sex, I know . . .
LISA	I was going to say, so clinical . . .

RICHIE   Clinical?

LISA   Like all you want is power over them . . .

RICHIE   You gotta have goals. You gotta have ambition. Else people think you're a cunt. They look right through you. (*Beat*.) It's like on the tube. You know when you're on the tube, and you look up, and someone's been looking at you? People just know. It's like something you give off. (*Beat*.) You know what I mean?

(*He looks intently at* LISA. *She gives nothing back*.)

(*getting up*) I found this photo.

LISA   What photo?

RICHIE   (*going to mantelpiece*) This morning, on the mantelpiece. I mean it's always been there, it's just I never looked at it . . .

LISA   Show me . . .

(*He brings the photo back to the sofa. Sits back down. A little bit closer than before.*)

RICHIE   That's you. With the black hair . . .

LISA   Congratulations . . .

RICHIE   And Switch. Without the beer gut . . .

LISA   Very good . . .

RICHIE   But who's this? With the cheekbones? Geezer giving you the eye?

(*Beat*.)

LISA   Richie?

RICHIE   What?

LISA   Would you mind, like . . . not sitting quite so
              close?

RICHIE   What?

LISA   Would you mind kind of . . . moving up a bit?

              (*Beat.*)

RICHIE   Sure. (*Beat.*) No problem.

LISA   Nothing personal, eh?

              (*An awkward silence. He gets up, puts the
              photo back on the mantelpiece.*)

RICHIE   Do you want a tea, or a coffee?

              (*Beat.*)

LISA   I want to know what's going on.

RICHIE   What do you mean?

LISA   You know what I mean. This morning, OK, I
              get up for a pee. I bump into Switch, just as
              he's leaving. He's wearing sandals, a Jesus
              shirt, and his face is covered in sticking
              plaster. Now what the fuck is all that about?

RICHIE   Why don't you ask him?

LISA   Because the answer would take half an hour,
              contain references to the Bible and James
              Brown, and leave me none the wiser at the end
              of it. Much simpler just to ask you.

              (RICHIE *has moved to the window. Pause.*)

RICHIE   Look. How much do you know?

LISA   Enough.

RICHIE   Like the basics?

LISA   I know what he does.

                (*Pause.*)

RICHIE   He found out if you're on sickness – like if
                you're disabled, or schizophrenic, or whatever
                – they just pay everything straight into your
                account. You don't even have to leave the
                house . . .

LISA   So he, signing on as . . .

RICHIE   Julian Marshall.

LISA   . . . is now pretending that Julian Marshall is
                insane?

RICHIE   It's like the jackpot. Jobseeker's, Housing and
                Sickness. He reckons once it's up and running
                – like, aliases in every borough, people around
                the country, he can make fifty, seventy grand
                a year. And that's just him.

                (LISA *takes it in.*)

LISA   And what about you?

RICHIE   What about me?

LISA   What do you reckon?

RICHIE   If it's there, take it.

LISA   Simple as that.

RICHIE   Just do it.

LISA   What if everybody did it?

RICHIE   What if everybody wore the same colour shirt?
            It's not gonna happen, is it? (*Beat.*) Look,
            everyone's shafting someone. That's how it is.
            Mostly it's you getting shafted – like with
            taxes, or the stuff they put in your food, make
            more money out of you. (*Beat.*) You do what
            you can. (*Beat.*) It's like . . . round here . . .
            they don't even have banks. It's not worth it.
            Without the scammers there'd be nothing. No
            shops, no pubs. Nobody playing music. It's
            how things work. And they know that.
            Otherwise we'd be round their place, torching
            their houses, looting their stuff . . .

LISA   How many people?

RICHIE   Twenty, thirty.

LISA   *Thirty* different people.

RICHIE   It's all over there. On computer. I do the
            books.

            (LISA *absorbs this.*)

LISA   So take me through it. The average day.

RICHIE   (*shrugs*) There isn't one.

LISA   Alright, yesterday. Before I arrived.

            (RICHIE *thinks, then matter-of-factly outlines
            the schedule.*)

RICHIE   Up at 6 o'clock, drive to Manchester. Sign on
            at 9.30. Quick breakfast in Fallowfield, then
            M62 to Liverpool, sign on Sefton Park at
            11.00. Sorry we're late, had to take sick mum
            to hospital. Couple of pints in the pub, back
            on the M6, stop off in Brum for afternoon
            driving test, then back in N15 for 4 o'clock.

LISA   Driving test.

RICHIE   (*obvious*) For the ID.

                  (*Before* LISA *can answer, we hear the sound of
                  the door opening, off. Enter* SWITCH, *who
                  sweeps into the room in a state of happy
                  agitation. He is carrying a bottle of
                  champagne, and is dressed as in Scene One,
                  but with plasters on both face and hands.*)

SWITCH   (*mock rhetorical*) I have a dream. (*Beat.*) A
                  nation of fruitcakes. A country full of crazies.
                  A schizophrenic in every home. (*Beat.*) Tough
                  on work. Tough on the causes of work. Truly
                  we in Britain have never had it so good . . .

                  (*With this he releases the cork in the
                  champagne bottle. There is a loud pop.*)

                  What's the matter with you two?

                  (*Blackout.*)

                            Scene Four

SWITCH, LISA, TARA *and* RICHIE *are sitting at a street table
outside an expensive Soho restaurant. The end of a long and
indulgent day.*

SWITCH   You don't have to be some hippie arsehole to
                  see that everything that's out there –
                  everything there is to do, or see, or eat, or
                  snort – the only reason it exists is for you to
                  buy it. You either make shit or you eat it . . .

LISA   Oh, come on . . .

SWITCH   I mean pop tarts. The guy that invented pop
                  tarts. Or strawberry condoms. Or the three-in-
                  one adjustable shower nozzle. Does he get up
                  in the morning, throw open the bedroom
                  window and think, before me there was only
                  this, this *nothing*, this *void*? (*Beat.*) Now
                  people have the *freedom*, people have the *right*

to enjoy my . . . my zingy fruit and waffle
combination breakfast cereals . . .

LISA   You're saying those things aren't worth
            having?

SWITCH   Are you saying they are?

LISA   And the thousands of people who make them,
            the people that innocently buy them – they're
            worthless too?

SWITCH   I just don't see the point . . .

LISA   The point of what?

SWITCH   Of going to school, of *learning* things . . . you
            know . . . *liquids* . . . *solids* . . . The Fall of
            the Roman *Empire* . . . I don't see the point of
            all that, if you're just going to do something
            vulgar and meaningless at the end of it . . .

LISA   There are other things . . .

SWITCH   Look, in twenty years time there won't even
            be jobs. Just Rupert, Bill, and then the rest of
            us. Seven billion scroungers, camped outside
            their gates.

            (*Beat.*)

LISA   Tara, what are you working on at the moment?

TARA   A couple of things. (*Beat.*) Nothing definite.
            This friend of mine's written a play. He's
            getting some people to read it . . .

LISA   Where's that?

TARA   At a pub in Highbury . . .

LISA   Is it a good play?

TARA   Yes. I think so . . .

LISA   What's it about?

TARA   It's set in a bar. About these people who work
                there. These actors and musicians . . .

LISA   What about the money?

TARA   The money?

LISA   Is it good money?

TARA   Not exactly . . .

SWITCH   What she means is, it's no money at all. Rien
                de fuck all. Which is why she's working for
                me . . .

                (TARA *gives him a look*.)

                Isn't it?

                (*Beat*.)

SWITCH   In fact . . .

TARA   What?

SWITCH   I was just thinking . . .

                (*Pause*. SWITCH *looks at* LISA.)

TARA   What?

                (*Beat*.)

LISA   (*shaking head*) Uh-uh.

SWITCH   You don't know what I was thinking.

LISA   Chat people up in pubs? Steal their identities?

SWITCH   Why not?

LISA   I don't think so . . .

SWITCH   In the old days you'd've jumped at it . . .

LISA   In the old days I'd've climbed that lamp-post,
            drunk, in fishnets and stilettos. I wouldn't do
            that again either.

SWITCH   We need more names . . .

LISA   So you do it. Or him . . .

SWITCH   'Owing to recent rapid expansion, British
            Fraud PLC is seeking to recruit young,
            ambitious field researchers. 30K per annum
            realistic earnings . . . '

            (*Pause.*)

LISA   (*laughs*) You're serious.

SWITCH   Maybe. Maybe not.

LISA   You honestly expect me to sit in some seedy
            pub, allow myself to be chatted up by drunken
            strangers, then offer to read their palms?

SWITCH   Think of it as a holiday job. (*Beat.*) Now . . .

            (*He bangs the wine bottle down on the table.*)

            I have in my pocket the sum of one thousand
            pounds. Half of that sum I have decided to
            donate to Mum's Wheelchairs for Disabled
            Sheepdogs charity. The other half – the
            remaining five hundred pounds – it is our task
            to spend before ten o'clock tonight.

TARA   I'm fucked.

RICHIE   Me too.

LISA   Look, even you can't blow five hundred
            pounds in fifty minutes.

SWITCH   Wanna bet?

LISA   No.

SWITCH   (*hailing an extremely tired-looking* WAITER)
Waiter . . .

WAITER   (*approaching*) Sir?

SWITCH   We'd like a bottle of brandy.

WAITER   Yes, sir. The house brandy?

SWITCH   Is that expensive?

WAITER   Sir?

SWITCH   I said, is that expensive?

WAITER   The Remy Martin is forty-nine pounds and
fifty pence.

SWITCH   Bring me a bottle of the most expensive
brandy you have.

(*Beat.*)

WAITER   That would be the Marcel Trepou. 1955. An
Armagnac.

SWITCH   How much is that?

WAITER   Seven hundred and forty-two pounds, ninety-
seven pence. Plus VAT.

SWITCH   Excellent. We'll have a bottle of that.

WAITER   Yes, sir.

SWITCH   Oh, and waiter. Four glasses.

(*He goes. A stunned silence.*)

RICHIE   Jesus, Switch.

TARA   I can't believe you just did that.

SWITCH   How can I put it? If you're gonna *eat* shit, you
            might as well eat the most expensive shit in
            the world. (*An awkward silence. To* TARA)
            What's up?

TARA   Everyone's staring.

SWITCH   You're an actress. You're supposed to like
            that.

            (*A further awkward silence.*)

TARA   I don't even *like* brandy.

SWITCH   (*northern accent*) This is *my* party, and you'll
            drink what you're given.

            (*Beat.*)

LISA   So, Tara. What would happen if you *didn't*
            read this play?

TARA   Sorry?

LISA   What if you just said, thanks, but no thanks,
            I've got better things to do with my time?

SWITCH   She'd be lying . . .

TARA   (*ignoring him*) Better things than what?

LISA   Than reading a play for no money . . .

TARA   (*shrugs*) Someone else'd do it.

LISA   And if they didn't?

TARA   Someone else would . . .

            (*Pause.*)

LISA   So what you're saying is . . . there's a more or less bottomless well of out-of-work actors prepared to do this job for no money?

TARA   What are you getting at?

              (*Enter* WAITER *with bottle and glasses.*)

LISA   Richie, what about you?

RICHIE   What about me?

LISA   How much did you get for this gig the other night?

RICHIE   How much?

LISA   I'm just curious.

RICHIE   It was a showcase . . .

LISA   So you worked for nothing?

RICHIE   You've got to see it as an investment. Sort of a long-term thing.

LISA   And in the meantime?

RICHIE   I get by.

              (*Beat.*)

TARA   What are you trying to say?

LISA   I don't know.

TARA   Go on. Spit it out.

              (*Beat.*)

LISA   It's like . . . .the other day, as we were coming into Heathrow, I was thinking, actually, wouldn't it be *fantastic* to have a job?

RICHIE   A job?

LISA   Wouldn't it be great if, on Monday morning,
                tanned and refreshed by my two weeks in
                Tunisia, I could simply turn up somewhere,
                sort out the blue forms from the pink ones,
                then bugger off home. To my flat in Maida
                Vale. And my bottle of Chardonnay . . .

RICHIE   Sounds like hell.

LISA   I don't think it does.

TARA   So what are you saying?

LISA   I told you. I don't know . . .

TARA   You think I'm wasting my time?

LISA   Do you?

TARA   That's what you're implying.

LISA   You said it. Not me . . .

                (SWITCH *attracts the attention of the* WAITER.)

WAITER   Is everything OK, sir?

SWITCH   Everything's fine. Absolutely fine.

WAITER   Would you like the bill?

SWITCH   Yes – I think this would be a good moment.
                Thank you.

                (*Lights fade.*)

Scene Five

The living room. Three o'clock in the morning.

SWITCH *plays a simple melody on an electric keyboard – a
doodle, something he is trying to work out.*

Enter LISA.

LISA   This place is filthy.

SWITCH   I'll make some tea.

LISA   How long has this glass been here?

SWITCH   When it gets unbearable I get someone in.

LISA   Why don't you do it?

SWITCH   I don't have the time . . .

LISA   You have all the time in the world. How could
            you possibly need *more* time?

            (SWITCH *carries on doodling.* LISA *lights a
            cigarette.*)

LISA   I'm sorry about before.

SWITCH   Why did you just fuck off?

LISA   You were treating that guy like a cunt.

SWITCH   He was pissed. He was hitting on Tara.

LISA   The guy walks into a cab office, sits down
            next to you two – next thing he knows he's
            had his palm read and his ID stolen.

SWITCH   You wound her up. She was just trying to
            prove something.

LISA   Yeah, well he never deserved that.

            (*Pause.* SWITCH *carries on playing.*)

LISA   What is that?

SWITCH   This?

LISA

Sounds familiar . . . like the start of
something. Or the harmony . . .

SWITCH

Something I made up.

(*He carries on playing.*)

LISA

(*sudden outburst*) This is so *stupid*.

SWITCH

What is?

LISA

You are the most naturally gifted person I
have ever met. No question. There is nothing
in the world you could not do.

SWITCH

Like what?

LISA

Like anything.

SWITCH

Why bother? Why be a second-rate . . .
whatever . . . when you can be the most
talented benefit fraudster of your generation?

LISA

But that's like saying . . . don't get out of bed
unless you can be Beethoven or . . . Prime
Minister.

(SWITCH *picks out a new melody.*)

SWITCH

What about this?

LISA

Listen, will you?

(*He stops.*)

SWITCH

Alright. I'm listening.

(*Beat.*)

LISA

I spoke to your mum . . .

SWITCH

In Sweden?

LISA   She phoned my mum. Mum phoned the tour
                manager. I spoke to her last week. (*Beat.*)
                She's worried, Steve.

SWITCH   What about?

LISA   This. Everything. She hears nothing for
                months on end. What she does hear scares her
                stupid. If you needed money for bail . . . or
                whatever . . . she'd have to put up the house.
                Her home. And you know she's daft enough to
                do that.

                (*Pause.*)

SWITCH   You got any skins?

                (*Beat.*)

LISA   (*exasperated*) Just tell me one thing.

SWITCH   What?

LISA   What is the difference between this . . .

SWITCH   What?

LISA   Freebasing coke, pretending to be *mad* for a
                living . . .

SWITCH   And?

LISA   What do you think?

                (*Beat.*)

SWITCH   You think I'm going to piss myself for real?
                Like the guy in Colditz?

LISA   I'm serious.

SWITCH   It's a buzz. A hit.

LISA   What is?

SWITCH	Spend a few hours inside someone else's head.
LISA	I don't understand.

(*Beat.*)

SWITCH	Tomorrow I am Anthony Fisher. Freelance photographer. With a flat in Dean Street. And a seafront house in Brighton. Anthony wears Gautier and Agnes B. He has a taste for silk underwear, a bulging address book, and a repetitive strain injury . . .
LISA	What are you on about?
SWITCH	Yesterday I was Terry Newman. Unemployed drifter. My father used to drink, used to slap me around the house. He taught me about pain, about the meaning of violence. Hit first, hit hard, don't ask questions.
LISA	What are you saying?
SWITCH	You should try it. It's therapeutic.

(*There is something a bit scary about this. Outside we hear the sound of a dustbin lid crashing to the ground.*)

LISA	(*startled*) What's that?
SWITCH	I dunno. Just a cat.

(*Beat.* LISA *regains her composure.*)

LISA	Are you seeing anyone?
SWITCH	You mean a shrink?
LISA	I meant a woman . . .
SWITCH	The usual. Drunken brunettes. Mad foreign girls . . .

LISA   So not Tara . . .

              (*Beat.*)

SWITCH   I get bored . . .

LISA   That's because they're boring.

SWITCH   Happy brunettes are all alike. Each unhappy
              brunette is unhappy in her own way.

              (LISA *laughs, in spite of herself. Enter* RICHIE.)

RICHIE   There's a man outside. He was there when we
              got back. He's still there now. I think that was
              him knocked over the bin.

              (SWITCH *goes to the window. Gently pulls back
              the blind. Purses his lips.*)

SWITCH   Where?

RICHIE   Over on the other side of the road. Standing
              by the newsagent.

SWITCH   I can't see anyone.

              (RICHIE *approaches the window. Looks out.*)

RICHIE   Blue bomber jacket, short hair. About thirty-
              five.

LISA   Is the back door locked?

SWITCH   I'll double-lock it.

LISA   Yeah . . .

SWITCH   Relax. Everything's fine . . .

              (*Lights fade.*)

ACT ONE

Scene Six

The living room. The following evening.

SWITCH *is in his chair. In full flow.* RICHIE *is by the window,
trying to see out without being seen.*

SWITCH   Your great grandparents hew rocks, or catch
                    fish. Your grandparents sell things, or make
                    them. Your parents use their brains . . . have
                    aspirations . . . . Then *you* get sent to college,
                    where you study a poet who drank absinthe,
                    kept a lobster on a string, and made a living
                    out of *despising* people like your parents.
                    (*Pause.*) You learn the entire history and
                    geography of Bohemia – who took what, where
                    they took it, blah blah blah blah blah – and
                    then – what? – you're supposed to just . . . *un-*
                    think these things? Do something *useful*?
                    (*Beat.*) Clogs to clogs in four generations.
                    That's what my Gran used to say. It's like my
                    dad. I mean . . . I remember all this
                    excitement. When we were kids. When they
                    wiped out some disease. Smallpox or scrofula
                    or whatever. I remember the passion. And the
                    certainty. That we could go on doing this.
                    That all the . . . *bad* things in the world could
                    be fixed. That humanity – armed with its
                    sword of Progress, its shield of Commerce –
                    would go marching on – ever onwards – into
                    the bright sunlit dawn of the future. (*Beat.*)
                    But it's like, who believes that now? Who
                    honestly believes that now? (*Beat.*) What are
                    you doing?

RICHIE   Nothing. You shouldn't listen to her.

SWITCH   What?

                    (*Pause.*)

RICHIE   What fucking right has she got? Going on like
                    that?

(*Pause.* SWITCH *registers* RICHIE'S *hostility.*
Enter LISA, *flushed, with shopping bags and*
flowers.)

SWITCH   Hi.

RICHIE   I'm gonna wash my trousers.

SWITCH   Where've you been?

              (RICHIE *exits without looking at* LISA.)

LISA   Out on the marshes. I just walked and walked.
              Till it got dark . . .

SWITCH   What's in the bags?

LISA   Fresh meat. Fresh fruit. Fresh vegetables.

SWITCH   What for?

LISA   I'm going to cook.

SWITCH   What about the flowers?

LISA   The flowers are for you.

SWITCH   Why?

              (*Suddenly she approaches, and without*
              warning, kisses SWITCH *on the cheek.*)

LISA   Because I would like to spend *one* civilised
              evening with my oldest friend in the world.
              Any objections?

              (SWITCH *is too surprised to reply.*)

              (*looking for a container for the flowers*) What's
              he doing?

SWITCH   I don't know. You could ask him.

              (*Beat.*)

LISA	Its funny. Listening to Richie.
SWITCH	Why funny?
LISA	Like listening to you. Way back when. Only somehow . . . diluted.
SWITCH	You don't like him.
LISA	He's a boy.
SWITCH	But you don't like him . . .
LISA	I don't have . . . any opinion.

(SWITCH *thinks*.)

SWITCH	A boy . . .

(*Beat.*)

LISA	How was today?
SWITCH	Today?
LISA	Today was . . . Anthony Fisher. The photographer?

(*Pause.*)

SWITCH	Look . . .
LISA	What?

(SWITCH *thinks better of whatever he was going to say.*)

SWITCH	I'll get you something.
LISA	No, what?
SWITCH	For the flowers.

RICHIE   (*off, but sotto voce*) Switch . . .

SWITCH   What?

RICHIE   He's here.

SWITCH   Who is?

RICHIE   Blue jacket. Crew cut.

              (SWITCH *frowns.*)

              From last night.

SWITCH   What's he doing?

RICHIE   He's coming up the path.

              (*There is a loud and sustained buzzing at the
              front door.* SWITCH *goes off. Opens the door.
              There is the sound of a brief struggle in the
              hallway.*)

SWITCH   (*off*) Who the fuck are you?

LISA   Switch?

              (*Enter* MAN. *Thirty-fiveish. Fit. Cropped hair.
              His right hand is bandaged.* SWITCH *follows.
              The* MAN *looks round the room.* SWITCH *goes
              to the phone.*)

MAN   I wouldn't bother with that.

LISA   Who is this?

MAN   I said down. Put the phone down.

              (*The* MAN *makes a sudden move towards* LISA,
              twisting her arm viciously behind her back.
              LISA *almost beside herself with fear.* SWITCH
              slowly puts down the phone.)

              That's it.

LISA   What do you want?

                (*The* MAN *releases* LISA.)

MAN   Over there. On the sofa. Both of you . . .

                (*They start to move.*)

SWITCH   There's no money . . .

MAN   No?

SWITCH   A few quid. TV, video. Take the lot . . .

                (*They are now sitting on the sofa.*)

MAN   Now. You are? (*Beat.*) Again? (*Still no reply.*)
                I said I didn't catch the name.

SWITCH   Look, just take the gear and fuck off, OK?
                What's it matter who we are?

MAN   Oh it matters to me. It matters a great deal. A
                person's identity. Who a person is . . .

SWITCH   Stephen.

MAN   Stephen who?

SWITCH   Stephen Waller.

MAN   As in Fats?

SWITCH   Very good.

MAN   And you are?

LISA   Lisa.

MAN   Say again?

LISA   Lisa. Lisa Fox.

MAN   You seem sort of familiar, Lisa. Why is that?

LISA   I don't know.

MAN   Are you on TV?

             (SWITCH *suddenly glances at the shrine on the mantelpiece. The photograph is of a man with long, straggly hair and a moustache. He looks back at the intruder.*)

SWITCH   Who are you? And what do you want?

             (*Pause. The* MAN *says nothing.*)

SWITCH   This is about the TV license . . .

MAN   Very good. (*Beat.*) You see that's what you miss. When you're away. The English sense of humour . . .

SWITCH   You've been away . . .

MAN   I've been all over. Hong Kong, Saudi. The Emirates. Last three years I've been in Berlin. (*Beat.*) You should go there, Stephen. And you, Lisa. It's another world out there. Like the Wild West. The Wild East.

             (*Beat.*)

             See, a bunch of us went out there. English brickies and chippies. Building brothels on the Polish border. Tell you what, it's unreal. Grand, two grand a week. You can do anything. Booze, drugs, women. Caviare for breakfast. Anna Kournikova sitting on your face for a fiver . . .

SWITCH   So why did you leave?

MAN   Well, this is my point, Stephen. This is what I'm getting to. You see I'm a bit old-fashioned. A bit of a traditionalist. What I believe is – you can have too much of a good thing . . .

SWITCH   Yeah?

MAN   Don't you agree?

          (SWITCH *shrugs*.)

          'Cos if we're living for pleasure, Stephen – if we can have whatever we want, whenever we want it, what are we? Mmm? We're no better than animals, are we? (*Beat*.) Without hope. Without aspiration. (*Beat*.) Where was I?

SWITCH   On the Polish border.

MAN   So. We've been there eighteen months or so. Building these brothels. Summer's turning to autumn, leaves are falling off the trees, and I'm thinking to myself, I'm starting to think, this is not how I want to live. This is not how I want to live my life. I'm thinking pubs. I'm thinking football. I'm thinking house. I'm thinking married. I'm thinking time to get married. Time to settle down. Time to take stock . . .

LISA   So what's stopping you?

          (*Beat*.)

MAN   Last night we were there, we had this party. This massive celebration to open one of the cathouses. Champagne was flowing, girls from all over, cake the shape of a dick with a Boris Yeltsin face. Then all of a sudden . . . it's midnight, glasses are raised, clock's about to strike . . . in walk the boys.

SWITCH   What boys?

MAN   The local wiseguys. The mafia. (*Beat*.) For a split second it's quiet. Deathly quiet. Then it's

mayhem. Bottles, glasses, mirrors. Everything
smashed to fuck. Then what?

SWITCH   I don't know.

MAN   You know what happened next?

SWITCH   Tell us.

MAN   One by one they go up to the British lads. The
              brickies. The chippies. The roofers. And they
              get us to hold out our hands. And then one at
              a time – knuckle by knuckle, finger by finger
              – they smash our hands to pieces with the
              butts of their guns . . .

SWITCH   Why did they do that?

MAN   (*obvious*) Because the builders used Brits.
              Instead of the local Polack meatheads. So
              when I get back, I go to the doctor. He takes
              one look, and he says to me, 'it'll set – but
              it'll never be right.' I says, what do you mean?
              He says 'he hopes I can saw left-handed.' I
              tell him no. He says 'well either you learn, or
              you start looking for a new job. In the
              meantime here's your sickie for the Social . . . '

SWITCH   Terry Newman.

NEWMAN   So I go to the Social and they say 'there must
              be some mistake'. I says what? 'You're
              already signed on. In fact you're due for a
              Restart on Tuesday.' I says what? 'Look it
              says here, Tuesday morning.' I say of course.
              Silly me. What time is that again? (*Beat.*) So I
              waited. On Tuesday morning. Till I went in.
              Then after it was over I followed myself home.
              To this house. Where I used to live . . .

SWITCH   What do you want?

NEWMAN   You and I should step out. Shouldn't we?
               Have a little chat. I remember the beer at the
               Askil's not too bad.

               (SWITCH *looks at* LISA.)

               Shall we?

               (SWITCH *looks back at* NEWMAN. *Blackout.*)

               Scene Seven

The living room. Later that evening.

LISA   So where's he gone now?

RICHIE   See this friend, owes him some money.

LISA   Which friend?

RICHIE   Just a friend.

LISA   Five thousand pounds by next Monday.
               Where's he gonna get five thousand pounds?

RICHIE   Lot of people owe him stuff. One way or
               another . . .

LISA   How come?

RICHIE   Just people he's helped. Given them money . . .

LISA   This is Tara? (*Beat.*) He's gone to see Tara,
               right?

RICHIE   How do I know?

LISA   Why the big secret?

               (*Beat.*)

RICHIE   Why don't you ask him? Look. He knows you
               think she's a waste of space. That's why.

LISA   I don't understand.

RICHIE   (*shrugs*) She gets to call herself an actress, he
              gets to . . . whatever. Anyway – her dad's
              loaded. He's gone to see if she can borrow the
              cash. Like an emergency loan . . .

LISA   If Daddy's loaded, how come he doesn't pay
              the bills?

RICHIE   Because *he* thinks she's earning. He thinks
              she's a real actress. Like, when she does one
              of these pub gigs, she's actually getting some
              money . . .

LISA   So what's she going to say?

RICHIE   How do I know? She needs her teeth fixed,
              silicone implants, whatever . . .

              (*Pause.* LISA *lights a cigarette.*)

LISA   I don't believe this.

RICHIE   What?

LISA   All his life it's been like this. The same room.
              The same chair. The same idiotic wheezes and
              scams. The same cast of sniggering acolytes.
              Building him up. Egging him on. The ugly kid
              with the big feet who'd do anything to get
              attention.

RICHIE   What?

LISA   Then the shit hits the fan – teacher comes in
              while he's blowing up the condom, he gets
              caught robbing the college bar – and where
              are you? Fucking nowhere, that's where.

RICHIE   What are you talking about?

LISA   Oh, come on . . .

RICHIE   I didn't make him like this. Nobody did.

LISA   Down the pub with your pals. 'My mate
              Switch, King of The Scams.' Gives you a little
              buzz, doesn't it?

RICHIE   You got this all wrong.

LISA   But when the going gets tough . . .

RICHIE   What do you mean?

LISA   Like just now..

RICHIE   What do you mean?

LISA   Three against one maybe he'd've backed
              off . . .

RICHIE   You're saying I bottled it?

LISA   I'm saying how could you just sit there and do
              nothing?

RICHIE   It was three against a psycho. That's still
              pretty lousy odds as far as I'm concerned.
              (*Beat.*) Look, what is your problem?

              (*They are very close. There is a charge
              between them. Off stage, the front door bell
              rings.*)

LISA   Shit.

RICHIE   What? (*He goes to the window, looks out.*)
              Some geezer in a leather coat.

              (RICHIE *starts to go off.* LISA *frowns.*)

LISA   Wait.

              (RICHIE *checks.*)

              What sort of leather coat?

RICHIE	I dunno, a leather coat.
LISA	Short? Long?
RICHIE	Long.
LISA	Hair colour?
RICHIE	Sorry?

(*Another ring of the bell.*)

LISA	Hair colour?
RICHIE	Dark.
LISA	OK Richie, I want you to do something.
RICHIE	Look, what is this?
LISA	I want you to stop there, exactly where you are, and I want you to stay there till I tell you otherwise.

(*A prolonged ring of the bell.*)

RICHIE	Why?
LISA	Without making a sound.

(*Beat.* RICHIE *goes to speak.*)

I said without breathing.

(*Another prolonged ring. Followed by some short ones. Followed by the sound of something smashing. Followed by silence. When it is quite certain that* LEATHER COAT *has departed,* RICHIE *finally exhales.*)

RICHIE	What was all that about?
LISA	Let's just say there's someone I'm not that keen to talk to just at this moment.

(RICHIE *thinks*.)

RICHIE   Danny. Danny Garratt . . . .

LISA   Richie, I take it all back. You're the finest human being that ever lived.

RICHIE   Does this mean you quit the band?

(LISA *thinks. Maybe that is what it means. But before she can reply, we hear the sound of the side door shutting offstage.* SWITCH *surges in, his arms full of stuff from the late night garage. Pringles, Ferrero Rocher, etc.*)

SWITCH   Sorted.

RICHIE   Yeah?

SWITCH   No worries.

LISA   You mean Daddy's sending a cheque?

(SWITCH *flashes a glance at* RICHIE, *who gives him a helpless shrug.*)

SWITCH   Backbone of England, his sort. Always said it.

LISA   So is he?

SWITCH   Now . . .

LISA   Switch . . .

SWITCH   Pringles? Ferrero Rocher?

LISA   Is he sending a cheque?

(*Beat.* LISA *looks* SWITCH *in the eye.*)

SWITCH   Look can we talk about this tomorrow?

(*Blackout.*)

END OF ACT ONE

ACT TWO

Scene One

The living room. Next morning. SWITCH *hammering, fitting a lock on the window.* RICHIE *loafing, reading music paper.* (*Sub headline on paper: BLUE ROSES: GARRATT AND FOX GO AWOL IN UPPSALA*)

SWITCH   I was reading this thing. Couple of weeks back. This guy – this Bob Dylan fan – he'd written an article about all the times Bob mentions the word 'window' in his songs.

RICHIE   What are you on about?

SWITCH   I was just thinking window . . . you know . . . and I was thinking . . . this bloke . . . this *accountant* . . . he's sat down, he's listened to twenty-eight different albums, forty-six bootlegs and a couple of dozen pirate CDs, and he's worked out all the different meanings of the word 'window' in the oeuvre of Bob Dylan. He's worked out when it means opportunity, as in window of, he's worked out when it means vagina, as in 'open up and let me in', and he's worked out when it just means window . . .

RICHIE   As in wooden frame containing pane of glass?

SWITCH   Exactly.

RICHIE   And?

SWITCH   And I just thought . . . you know . . . dressing up in sandals . . . drooling all over the dole office . . . it's not even close, is it?

RICHIE   You're sweating.

                  (SWITCH *stops hammering.*)

SWITCH	I've got these pains. In my stomach. Kept me awake all night.
RICHIE	You should go out. Get some air.
SWITCH	I'm lying there on the sofa. All this stuff running around in my brain. This problem, that problem. I just can't *focus*. You know? Every time I get close to something . . . to like some appreciation of things . . . bam . . . in it comes. All the usual shit. Names of Bond girls. Galton and Simpson sitcoms. Surviving Communist regimes . . .

(*Enter* LISA *with bag.*)

SWITCH	What's up?
LISA	I have to get out.
SWITCH	(*eyeing the bag*) Out where?
LISA	Just out.

(*She is trembling.*)

SWITCH	Lisa, what is it?

(*She says nothing.* RICHIE *gets up.*)

RICHIE	I'm gonna make some tea. Anyone want any?

(*Nobody answers.* RICHIE *shrugs and exits.*)

SWITCH	What's the matter?

(*Beat.*)

LISA	Switch, in two days' time you're going to be arrested. Or killed. Possibly both. And what are you doing?
SWITCH	I'm fitting a window lock.

LISA   Yeah, but what are you *doing*?

              (*Pause.*)

              It's like, what *is* this? How does it work?

SWITCH   How does what work?

LISA   Stuff We Want To Think About. Stuff We
              Don't Want To Know . . .

SWITCH   I don't understand.

LISA   You. Him. Every man I've ever known. (*Beat.*)
              I mean, why is it so hard to understand? You
              know? Cause and Effect. Action and Reaction.
              The basic fucking *physics* of things . . .

SWITCH   I'm lost.

LISA   Steal someone's identity, sooner or later that
              person's going to find out, be pretty upset.

SWITCH   I thought he was *dead* . . .

LISA   Open your doors to wasters and parasites,
              sooner or later those people are going to let
              you down. Big time.

SWITCH   Who is this?

LISA   Hang out with rent boy junkies, share their
              needles . . . sooner or later you're going to
              catch something, pass it on to someone . . .

SWITCH   What?

              (*Pause.*)

              Lisa?

              (*Pause.*)

              What happened?

LISA   You think you know someone. You think you
                  know someone pretty well. Their every
                  thought. Their every little kink. Then one day
                  you find out you don't. You don't know them
                  at all. You've been sharing your life with a
                  complete stranger . . .

SWITCH   This is Danny?

LISA   I walk into this bar. In Stockholm. I've been
                  to a gallery. All I want is a coffee and a sit-
                  down. Turns out it's the one place in
                  Stockholm you can score. In other words the
                  last place in the world I want to be. And there
                  he is. In the corner. With all these kids. One
                  needle between seven of them. We've been in
                  Sweden just under two hours, I've slipped out
                  to a gallery, and he, who gave up smack at the
                  same time as me, has been lying to me. For an
                  entire year. An entire year spent slipping away
                  like this, scoring off street kids in foreign
                  cities, using Christ knows what kind of shit . . .

SWITCH   Jesus.

                  (*A tear rolls down her cheek.*)

LISA   It's like if Iggy Pop did it, why not him?
                  What's the problem? We've all gotta go
                  sometime . . .

                  (*Pause. The tears now flowing freely.* SWITCH
                  goes to her. Hugs her tightly.)

SWITCH   Let's go away somewhere.

LISA   You're boiling.

SWITCH   Just get the fuck out of here.

LISA   Like a furnace.

SWITCH   That place in Wales . . .

LISA   Afterwards. We'll go away afterwards.

SWITCH   Where we grew the poppies.

LISA   I just need to know. One way or the other.

                (*Lights fade.*)

                          Scene Two

The living room. RICHIE *is at the decks, mixing. The music is
both intense and loud.*

Enter SWITCH, *wearing raincoat, glasses, plasters – but now
with Jesus shirt and sandals, too. Looking pretty wild.*

SWITCH   Turn it down.

RICHIE   What?

SWITCH   (*shouting*) I said turn the fucking music down.

                (RICHIE *does.*)

RICHIE   What's up?

SWITCH   I'm going to tell you a story.

RICHIE   (*puzzled*) OK.

SWITCH   I'm in the Restart interview. (*Beat.*)
                Everything's going fine. John of Patmos talks
                to me on buses, he's sending messages
                through the television. Blah, blah, blah, blah,
                blah. All of a sudden the guy leans over and
                says, 'I think you mean John the Redeemer.' I
                just look at him, try to stay in character. 'Also
                known as John of Goshen. A contemporary of
                Patmos, but much the more interesting
                character I always think.'

RICHIE   Fuck . . .

SWITCH	Turns out he's a New Testament scholar.
RICHIE	Jesus.
SWITCH	But that's by the by. That's not what I wanted to tell you.
RICHIE	(*vaguely uncomfortable*) No?
SWITCH	This is what I wanted to tell you.
RICHIE	What?
SWITCH	He tells me he doesn't know why he's doing this, but he kind of likes me. I remind him of a happy time in his life. A time before the drudgery of his current employment. (*Beat.*) So he opens the drawer, pulls out this piece of paper, and pushes it across the desk towards me.
RICHIE	What was on the paper?
SWITCH	A picture.
RICHIE	What picture?
SWITCH	A photofit picture. Of me. Not an exact likeness, of course. But me. Recognizably me.
RICHIE	I don't understand. They know who you are?
SWITCH	Not who I am. Just what I look like.
RICHIE	But how?
	(*Pause.*)
SWITCH	Well, that's where I thought you might be able to help.
RICHIE	Sorry?

SWITCH   I rather hoped you might be able to shed some light on that.

RICHIE   How?

(*Pause.*)

SWITCH   Richie, only a handful of people in the world know the detail on this. You. Me. Tara. A couple of other girls I used to read palms . . .

RICHIE   Everyone's got an idea . . .

SWITCH   But not the *detail*. How it's done. Where it's done. When it's done . . .

RICHIE   What are you saying?

SWITCH   Richie, have you ever talked to anyone?

RICHIE   No.

SWITCH   Some night in the pub. Or at a club.

RICHIE   Of course not.

SWITCH   Think. Think hard . . .

RICHIE   I wouldn't do that.

SWITCH   Wouldn't you?

RICHIE   Absolutely not.

SWITCH   What about Mike?

RICHIE   Mike who?

SWITCH   Mike Farrell . . .

(RICHIE *looks blank.*)

RICHIE   Who's Mike Farrell?

SWITCH   Also known as Slack. DJ Slack. From The
                Tunnel Club.

                (RICHIE *blenches*.)

                Ever talk to him?

RICHIE   Maybe once or twice. In passing . . .

SWITCH   What about?

RICHIE   This and that. Nothing . . .

SWITCH   What about his friend? Stuart? Ever talk to
                him?

RICHIE   Same as Mike. Couple of times. Maybe three.

SWITCH   Because you know what Stuart does, don't
                you?

RICHIE   Works in an office somewhere.

SWITCH   That's right. He works in an office. D'you
                know which office?

                (RICHIE *shrugs*.)

                Well I'll tell you, shall I? (*Beat*.) Stuart
                Lander works for the DSS. In Camden. Stuart
                Lander is Area Fraud Officer, Grade Seven,
                for the Boroughs of Camden and Islington.
                That's what Stuart Lander does.

                (RICHIE *is silent. Completely humiliated. There
                is a ring at the front door*.)

RICHIE   Look this could be anything. It might not even
                be you . . .

SWITCH   (*going to answer the door*) It was me, alright.
                Fucking *me*.

(RICHIE *is left to his despair. Re-enter* SWITCH, *followed by* TARA.)

TARA   That's the last time I go through anything like that. For anyone . . .

SWITCH   What happened?

TARA   I ended up going home. All the way to Wiltshire. Of course they're delighted to see me. Wonder how *The Seagull's* going . . .

RICHIE   You're in *The Seagull*?

TARA   Of course not. (*Beat.*) I ended up telling them I was *pregnant*. It's all been a ghastly mistake, can I borrow five thousand pounds for a private clinic and a holiday after the run?

SWITCH   Did they give you the money?

TARA   No. They absolutely didn't.

SWITCH   Shit.

TARA   Said how could I possibly make a decision like that before opening in a play?

SWITCH   So we're fucked.

TARA   No. You're fucked, I'm pregnant. And a liar . . .

SWITCH   Just not a very good one . . .

TARA   So you think of something. You're such a fucking genius . . .

(SWITCH *looks furious.*)

RICHIE   We could sell the story. You know – to a tabloid. 'My Life as a Dole Rat.' Change all the names . . .

SWITCH   Or we could cut you into small pieces, sell
              your vital organs to the Turks . . .

              (*Before* RICHIE *can react to this there is a loud
              buzz at the front door. Followed by a second,
              more violent bang. He goes off.*)

TARA   What's up?

RICHIE   Don't ask.

              (*We hear the front door open.*)

SWITCH   (*off*) Mr Newman . . .

NEWMAN   (*off*) Mind if I come in?

              (*Enter* NEWMAN, *now smartly – even
              fashionably – dressed, and carrying a hold-
              all. Followed by* SWITCH.)

              There's been a change of plan.

SWITCH   And you're here to tell us about it, is that
              right?

NEWMAN   Do you believe in destiny, Stephen? In a
              hidden hand, guiding us through life?

SWITCH   What do you want?

NEWMAN   I believe to every cloud there is a silver lining,
              if we could but see it. In every defeat there is
              the possibility of victory. Each end is in
              reality a new beginning, if we only choose to
              look at it that way. (*Beat.*) I'm leaving
              London tonight. And I'm leaving with that
              five thousand pounds. Plus –

              (*He pauses, takes in some of the hedonistic
              extravagance of the room.*)

              – another five.

(*Pause. An uncomfortable silence.*)

SWITCH   And if we haven't got it?

NEWMAN   Then I go straight to the Social. Tell them everything I know.

             (*Pause.*)

SWITCH   I don't understand.

NEWMAN   What's not to understand?

SWITCH   How does that benefit you?

NEWMAN   Sorry?

SWITCH   Going to the Social. How does that benefit you?

NEWMAN   I'm not sure I follow you.

SWITCH   If I'm banged up for fraud, how is that any use to you?

             (NEWMAN *advances. The others tense up.*)

NEWMAN   We had an agreement, Stephen.

SWITCH   (*retreating*) I'm serious.

NEWMAN   So am I.

SWITCH   You said five grand.

NEWMAN   Yeah well things change, don't they? Situations develop. Circumstances occur. And besides. (*Beat.*) That money's already spent . . .

             (*A long moment.*)

             (*icy*) If you don't give me the cash, then I simply take it. (*He looks round.*) TV, video,

car. *Then* I beat you senseless. *Then* I shag
your girlfriend. *Then* I go to the Social . . .

(NEWMAN *advances still further.* SWITCH *again
retreats, so that he is up against a set of
shelves at the edge of the room. His hand goes
behind him for balance.*)

SWITCH   (*quietly*) There's three of us. There's only one
of you . . .

TARA   Switch . . .

NEWMAN   Is that a threat?

TARA   He didn't mean anything . . .

NEWMAN   Are you threatening me, Stephen?

SWITCH   I said there's three of us and only one of you.
You gonna take us all at once or what?

(SWITCH'S *fingers tighten on something behind
him on the shelf. The iron.*)

NEWMAN   (*looking round*) Baby Spice, Posh Spice and
Old Spice. I'm pooing my pants, Steve . . .

SWITCH   Maybe you should be . . .

NEWMAN   I beg your pardon?

SWITCH   Maybe you should be . . .

(*Suddenly, and with surprising speed,* SWITCH
*swings the iron from behind his back, and
brings it crashing down on* NEWMAN'S *head.
The iron strikes him squarely on the temple,
and* NEWMAN, *wearing a brief look of utter
surprise, crumples to a heap on the floor. For
a second there is complete silence in the
room.*)

RICHIE   Fuck's sake . . .

TARA   Switch.

RICHIE   Jesus . . .

TARA   Are you OK?

              (SWITCH *is speechless. As if in a trance.*)

RICHIE   Look at this. He's spark out . . .

TARA   Switch?

              (RICHIE *approaches the body. Slaps* NEWMAN
              around the face.)

RICHIE   Dead to the world.

TARA   (*anxious*) Take his pulse.

RICHIE   What?

TARA   Take his pulse.

              (RICHIE *feels* NEWMAN'S *wrist.*)

RICHIE   Jesus.

TARA   What?

RICHIE   I can't feel anything.

              (*Enter* LISA. *She surveys the carnage of the
              flat.*)

LISA   What's going on? Someone?

              (*Blackout.*)

Scene Three

The living room. About twenty minutes later.

RICHIE, SWITCH, TARA, *and* LISA *consider the corpse lying on the ground.* SWITCH *is plainly agitated, but – for the moment – quiet.*

TARA   Only to me . . .

RICHIE   What?

TARA   Only to me could this happen.

RICHIE   It hasn't happened to you. It's happened to him. Hasn't it?

LISA   Looking at him there . . . it's so hard . . . like a child . . .

RICHIE   I was talking to this bloke. On the overground. Used to be a copper. He said the hardest thing was the bodies. You unroll the carpet, dig up the patio . . . dredge the boating lake. And then he said you try to picture them young. Sitting on swings. Smiling in paddling pools. He said you never, ever got used to it.

                (*A contemplative silence.*)

LISA   We should put him in something.

TARA   Like what?

LISA   I don't know. A sheet. Or a blanket.

TARA   Then what?

LISA   I don't know.

                (*A long silence.*)

RICHIE   Look, what *are* we going to do?

                (*Pause. Everyone realises they are looking to* SWITCH *for an answer.*)

SWITCH   I've been thinking.

(*Everyone turns, expectantly.*)

Nobody knows he's here.

LISA   How do you mean?

SWITCH   Nobody knows he's here in this house.

LISA   You mean nobody except us?

(*Pause. They consider this.*)

TARA   We don't know that.

SWITCH   Think about it. (*Beat.*) He came here to get
            money. Maybe rough somebody up. Who
            would he tell?

LISA   Anyone. A mate – someone in the pub . . .

SWITCH   I don't think so.

LISA   Why not?

SWITCH   The guy was a loner.

LISA   How can you know that?

SWITCH   You remember what he said. How he'd been
            away. Came back hoping to meet someone.
            Besides. He was sick. In the head. How many
            friends do you think a person like that's got?

TARA   Yeah, but today. All that stuff about fresh
            starts. New beginnings. Maybe he met
            someone.

SWITCH   Who though? Who would he meet?

TARA   A woman.

SWITCH   I don't think so.

TARA   Look at the clothes. Like he wanted to impress someone. Someone new . . .

(*Beat.*)

SWITCH   Even if that's true – even if he did meet someone – he's not gonna tell her about this. Is he?

(*Long pause.*)

LISA   So what are you saying?

(*Beat. Everyone absorbs the implications.*)

RICHIE   You mean . . . if a tree falls in the forest?

(*Pause.*)

LISA   Switch?

SWITCH   (*shrugs*) Nobody cared when he was alive. Why should anyone care now he's dead?

(*Long pause.*)

LISA   (*shocked*) You're talking about the life of a human being . . .

SWITCH   A meaningless life. A meaningless death.

LISA   You *killed* him . . .

SWITCH   It was an accident . . .

LISA   But he had no reason to be here. Did he? Except for what *you* did . . .

(*Beat.*)

SWITCH   So what's the alternative?

LISA   I don't believe this.

SWITCH	Tell me.
LISA	Someone, somewhere, will miss this person. If not this woman then a mother, or a brother . . .
SWITCH	Everything else means trouble. For all of us.
TARA	We could say he broke in, and it was self-defence . . .
SWITCH	And have the whole place crawling with CID? It's madness. Besides – he's been dead half an hour already . . .
RICHIE	You gotta admit . . .

(*Beat.*)

LISA	So you're saying if you remove the body – drop it in a lake, bury it in a wood – the whole problem simply ceases to exist?
SWITCH	What do you want me to do? Fall on my knees? Beg forgiveness? Turn myself in? It's done. It can't be undone . . .
LISA	I don't believe this . . .

(*She turns away. Goes to stand by the window.*)

SWITCH	Anyone got any better ideas?

(*There is no reply.*)

SWITCH	Right. Richie?
RICHIE	What?
SWITCH	Help me carry the body.
RICHIE	Where to?
SWITCH	The car.

RICHIE	You're joking . . .
SWITCH	I'm not joking.
RICHIE	It's broad daylight.
SWITCH	I'll back it up to the side-door. No one'll see us.
RICHIE	We can't.
SWITCH	We have to.
RICHIE	It's crazy.
SWITCH	So what do you suggest? We leave him in the cellar? Bury him under the patio?

(*Pause.*)

RICHIE	I can't, Switch. I just can't.
SWITCH	You owe me.
RICHIE	What?

(*Beat.*)

SWITCH	Forget it. (*He turns to* TARA.) Tara?
TARA	What?
SWITCH	(*meaning give him a hand*) What do you think?
TARA	This is absurd . . .
SWITCH	You think if you close your eyes and count to ten, the whole thing's just going to go away? You're as guilty as I am. Both of you are.

(*Beat.*)

TARA How'd you work that out?

SWITCH I pay your rent. I buy your food. He picked up the tab.

TARA We didn't kill him.

SWITCH So you'd've been happy just to stand here? Watch him beat me to a bloody pulp?

RICHIE He didn't mean that.

SWITCH That's how it sounded to me.

TARA He just wanted some money. Some kind of . . . compensation. Like you said, the guy had a shit life.

  (*A silence.*)

SWITCH (*suddenly*) Just go. All of you. Take your stuff and go.

RICHIE Switch –

SWITCH *Now.*

  (*No one has ever seen him like this before.
RICHIE and TARA wait for a second, then file,
in silence, from the room. LISA briefly meets
SWITCH's eye before she too leaves him, alone,
with the corpse. Slow fade.*)

Scene Four

Music: something spectral. Other-worldly.

*As the lights go up, the music segues into the sound of a Tony
Hancock audiotape – no more than a murmur – played on a
stereo somewhere in the room.*

SWITCH seems in another world.

SWITCH

I remember Dad used to tell us: in the old days
people were grateful. If you treated them. If
you treated their wives. They showed their
appreciation. Liked to give something back.
One patient he had, this guy worked for the
BBC. Back in the Fifties. Said he could get
Dad tickets for Hancock. Dad was ecstatic. In
his world Friday nights were sacred. You put
the world on hold for Tony. So off they go,
him and Mum, dressed to the nines, have the
night of their lives. Even get to meet the guy
afterwards. (*Beat.*) I know this because, years
later – I must have been about eleven years old
– they repeated the episode. Part of some
season of classic comedy on the BBC. Dad's
been going on about it for weeks. The one
about him and Sid – where they each think the
other one's trying to kill them. Anyway, down
we sit – me, my mum and dad and sister – and
immediately it starts I can hear it. The noise
we've been dreading. What Mum used to call
Dad's 'carrying laugh'. What me and my
sister used to call The Machine Gun. And, at a
distance of twenty-odd years and God knows
how many miles, I am embarrassed. Sweating
with embarrassment. At the open-hearted
bellow of the Hope Park slum doctor. (*Beat.*)
Then, just as we think it can't get any worse,
it does. My father starts to laugh. Some 1950s
kind of gag. And he just carries on laughing.
Soon other people are laughing. Laughing at
his laugh. And back it goes, forwards and
backwards, until – just when you think it's
never going to end – Hancock himself steps
in. Or rather seems to. He checks. In mid-
sentence. And you can almost hear him
thinking 'Oi – these people have come here to
listen to me, not to you. Put a sock in it.'
(*Beat.*) Afterwards, we're too embarrassed to
speak. It's like, nobody says a word – but we
all know who it was. It was our Dad. It was
his laugh. How are we ever going to show our
faces in public again? (*Beat.*) The other night
it was on again. On one of the satellites. And

as I watch I'm embarrassed all over again.
Embarrassed at my own eleven year-old
embarrassment. (*Beat.*) Because all I could
hear, as I listened to my father's
uncomplicated enjoyment, was the sound of
contentment. Of a man at ease with the world.
With who he was. With what he did. With
who he was married to. A man who – to cap it
all – was sitting in Broadcasting House with
complimentary tickets to watch the world's
greatest comedian at work. (*Beat.*) And I
thought to myself – I thought – that really is
as good as it gets.

(*As the music reasserts itself, the Hancock
fades into the background.* SWITCH *slowly gets
up. Has a good look round the flat. His world.
The universe he has created. It's over, and he
knows it. Slowly, he approaches the Shrine.
Newman's photo on the mantelpiece.
Deliberately, methodically, he detaches the
image from the frame. Considers the portrait
for a second. Then, taking his cigarette
lighter from his pocket, he ignites the paper,
waiting for it to catch. When it is alight, he
watches it burn, fascinated by the flames as
they curl upwards towards his fist. As he is
about to be scorched, he tosses the flaming
mess into the fireplace, where, as the lights
fade, he watches it slowly burn out. Blackout.*)

*In the darkness that now follows, the audience watches as the
room is transformed. Slowly stripped of all familiar artifacts
– ornaments, drug paraphernalia, recording studio – until the
effect is of a space dehumanised. A familiar room denuded of
all character or personality. And – by the deft addition of a
pair of glasses or the tying of the hair into a pony-tail – it's
as if* SWITCH *too is metamorphosed before the audience's very
eyes. Only* NEWMAN'S *corpse remains exactly as it was . . .*

As the lights go up a MAN *enters. He is about thirty-five, and
has the haircut of a policeman.*

SAVAGE   Who else lives in the house?

SWITCH   I told you. I hardly knew him. There was a
                kid, I think. But he moved out.

SAVAGE   And you came here . . .

SWITCH   I came here to look at the house. I heard he
                was leaving town. Needed to get things sorted.

SAVAGE   So what happened?

SWITCH   There was music. Coming from inside. I
                thought he mustn't have heard me knock.

SAVAGE   So you walked round the back of the house,
                where you observed Mr Newman through the
                rear window?

SWITCH   I knocked on the glass. Louder and louder. I
                thought he was asleep. And then I realised.

SAVAGE   At which point you broke the glass and gained
                entry to the house?

SWITCH   Yes.

                (*Pause.*)

SAVAGE   Mr Stephens, is there anyone you can think of
                might've wanted to do this to Mr Newman?

SWITCH   Like I say. I hardly knew him. (*Pause.*) He
                was a loner. Mixed with some pretty strange
                people.

SAVAGE   Can you think of the names of any of these
                people?

                (*He concentrates.*)

SWITCH   A big guy. Bit of a weirdo. I don't know his
                name. I heard they had a fight.

(*Beat.*)

SAVAGE You're absolutely sure you can't remember this person's name?

(*He thinks again.*)

SWITCH I'm sorry. I'm really bad with names.

(*Beat.*)

SAVAGE Mr Stephens. I get the very strong feeling there's something else you'd like to tell me.

(*Pause.* SWITCH *seems distracted.*)

SWITCH I don't think so.

(*Pause.*)

SAVAGE Is there any thing . . . any detail you feel you may have forgotten?

(*Pause.*)

SWITCH No . . .

SAVAGE You seem – if you don't mind me saying so – rather distracted.

SWITCH (*nervous laugh*) This is my first time. (*Beat.*) In the same room with a corpse.

(SAVAGE *looks* SWITCH *in the eye. Doesn't react to the joke.*)

SAVAGE Mr Stephens, I want you to think. To think extremely hard. About the identity of this person. The one you say may have quarrelled with Mr Newman. Is there anyone you know? Anyone close to you you think may also have been close to him?

(*Pause.* SAVAGE *continues to look intently at* SWITCH.)

SWITCH   Like I say. (*Beat.*) Our paths barely crossed.

SAVAGE   Think hard, Mr Stephens. Think very very hard.

              (*Pause.*)

SWITCH   I'm sorry.

              (*Beat.*)

SAVAGE   Very well. (*Beat.*) We'll obviously need to speak to you again.

SWITCH   Of course.

              (*Beat. A palpable tension.*)

SAVAGE   That address you gave me. (*Consulting notebook.*) Number sixteen, Auchinleck Road. Is that your permanent address?

SWITCH   It is.

SAVAGE   And you have no immediate travel plans?

SWITCH   Not that I can think of.

SAVAGE   In that case we'll be in touch Mr Stephens. (*Beat.*) As soon as we know what's what. (*Beat.*) I take it you can find your way out?

              (*The two men look each in the eye. Blackout.*)

Scene Five

A waiting room. In a clinic. The next day.

LISA *waits, fretfully.*

Enter SWITCH, *in the remains of his Mr Stephens costume.*

LISA   (*surprised*) How did you know where it was?

SWITCH   I looked in your bag. I'm sorry. The card was
                sticking out of the pocket.

LISA   It doesn't matter. I'm glad you came.

                (*Beat.*)

SWITCH   I hate these places. Always make you feel like
                you've done something wrong . . .

LISA   Wait till you see the nurse . . .

                (SWITCH *smiles. A wan smile. He sits down.*)

SWITCH   I wanted to explain.

LISA   About what?

SWITCH   What I said about . . . what happened . . .

LISA   Which part of it?

SWITCH   About him dying not mattering . . . (*Beat.*) I
                just . . . I don't know. It's like when you're a
                kid. And you've done something bad.
                Sometimes you say the worst thing that comes
                into your head. Just to distract people's
                attention, give them something else to think
                about . . .

                (*Beat.*)

LISA   So what happened?

SWITCH   You really want to know?

LISA   No. Actually I don't.

                (*Pause.*)

SWITCH	After it was over I drove to Wales. To that place. (*Beat.*) It seemed somehow appropriate. Morpheus. Morpheia. I slept in the car.
LISA	I just want this to be over.
SWITCH	I keep telling myself: this is a bad British movie – but that means it'll end, and then I can go home.
LISA	I've stopped dreaming. Nothing at all. It's like being dead.
	(*Pause.*)
SWITCH	Listen. I didn't just come here to hold your hand.
LISA	No?
SWITCH	I came here to ask you something.
LISA	What?
SWITCH	Not even ask, really. Make a suggestion . . .
LISA	Can't it wait?
SWITCH	I don't think so.
LISA	What then?
SWITCH	It's just I've been thinking. About what you've been saying . . .
LISA	About what?
SWITCH	About everything. About you, about me. Ever since you got back.
LISA	And?
SWITCH	I don't know how to say this . . .

LISA   Don't know how to say what?

            (*Beat. He can't get it out.*)

            Don't know how to say what?

            (*Enter* NURSE. LISA *looks up.* SWITCH *bites his lip.*)

NURSE   Would you like to come through?

            (LISA *exchanges a look with* SWITCH, *then gets up, walks on jelly legs toward the door. She exits with the* NURSE. LISA *is gone for what seems an eternity. Finally she returns, sits down where she was before.*)

LISA   Don't know how to say what?

SWITCH   What did she say?

LISA   Don't know how to say what?

            (*Beat.*)

SWITCH   I'd like us to live together.

LISA   Live together?

SWITCH   Get a house. Somewhere . . .

LISA   What do you mean?

SWITCH   I could get a job. Do something. You could . . . whatever . . . see how things work out.

            (*Beat.*)

LISA   You're saying you'd look after me?

SWITCH   I'm saying I think it would be good. For both of us.

LISA   You're saying you want to take on an invalid?

SWITCH   I'm saying you. I want to take on you.

                (LISA *absorbs what* SWITCH *has just said. She
                looks up at the No Smoking sign. Takes a
                cigarette out of the bag and lights it.*)

LISA   You remember the first time we met? At that
                awful Freshers' Fair? You got me drunk – a
                Fourth Year – took me back to your room. I
                thought you were trying to pick me up. Instead
                you played me all this music, read all that
                stuff to me out of books . . .

SWITCH   What stuff?

LISA   All that French stuff you were into. Guy
                Debord. Perpetual Novelty. The Situationist
                International . . .

SWITCH   You remember that?

LISA   That's what I loved about you. All that time
                we spent together. Never do the same thing
                twice. Never say the same thing twice. Never
                settle for less. That sense that you could re-
                invent the world. Go on re-inventing it. Day
                after day after day after day . . .

SWITCH   I said that?

LISA   You opened my eyes. My Croydon convent-girl
                eyes.

                (*Pause.* SWITCH *is embarrassed.*)

                But you know what? You know what I've come
                to realise? About the people who think like
                that?

SWITCH   What?

LISA   It's that ten years on – ten years down the line
                – they're the ones going: Everything's been

done. Everything's been said. Every
worthwhile thing has happened. (*Beat.*) And
yet still – somewhere – hoping someone's
going to walk into their lives, sprinkle them
with gold-dust, turn the base metal into
something precious.

SWITCH   That's what I'm saying . . .

LISA   And I just don't think I can live my life
around that. Not any more. It's like you –
Richie – Tara – not that you're the same as
them – you won't even get out of bed. Unless
you can be famous. Or rich. Or in some way . . .
extraordinary. (*Beat.*) Face it. You're
averagely bright. They're averagely stupid.

SWITCH   You told me I was the most gifted person
you'd ever met.

LISA   You *are*. The most gifted person *I've* ever
met. That doesn't make you Jonathan fucking
Miller, does it?

           (LISA *looks for somewhere to stub out her
           cigarette. Finally settles for the floor.*)

           Switch, look outside the door. At some of the
           casualties (*She gestures towards the window.*)
           on the other side of that window. You think
           they wouldn't give up *everything*? For even a
           fraction of what you've had. You think *they*
           think everything's been done?

           (*Beat.*)

SWITCH   So let's do it. (*Beat.*) Let's just go for it.

           (*Pause.*)

LISA   It's like Danny. All that stuff he comes out
           with. Miss Home and Garden. Miss Book at
           Bedtime. As if he was Miles fucking Davis. Or
           Jack Kerouac. Well, it's true. That's who I

am. Underneath the make-up. Before the
smack habit. And I'd just like to know –
what's so fucking wrong with that?

(*Pause.*)

SWITCH   I'm serious.

(*Pause.*)

LISA   I know you are. At this moment. And I'm
touched you had the idea. But that's it. Isn't
it? An idea. Something you haven't done. A
drug you haven't tried. What happens to me
when that drug wears off?

(*Enter* NURSE. *Sniffs the air disapprovingly.
Rearranges some magazines on the table.*)

NURSE   Not away celebrating?

LISA   We're just leaving.

(*Pause. The* NURSE *weighs up the situation.
Goes out.* SWITCH *absorbs the implications of
the* NURSE'S *remark.*)

SWITCH   Tell me one thing.

LISA   What?

SWITCH   If I'd asked you this five years ago, what
would you have said?

(*Beat.*)

LISA   (*sighs*) I'd've said no. And I'd've been a fool,
because yes . . . in my own way . . . not love
exactly . . . but *something* . . .

SWITCH   But not now?

LISA   Please can we have this conversation
somewhere else?

SWITCH	I just need to know . . .
LISA	What?
SWITCH	What it is that's changed . . .
LISA	I don't know. (*Beat.*) Lots of things. We're different people. You see things you never knew were there . . .
SWITCH	Like what?
LISA	Switch, a man is dead. You killed him. Can't you understand that? I don't know where that came from. And I don't think I want to. All I know is I looked at you, I looked at you and I thought . . . I don't know you. I don't know you at all. And that scared me.

(*Re-enter* NURSE.)

NURSE	We're locking up now.
LISA	We're just leaving.

(LISA *starts to go.*)

SWITCH	I'll catch you up.
LISA	Whatever.

(*She goes.* SWITCH *remains motionless. Utterly lost. Fade to black.*)

Scene Six

An anonymous bedsit. Possibly the home of Mr Stephens. Possibly not.

SWITCH *stands by the window. Half-dressed. Feet bare.* TARA *takes in the bleakness of the room.*

SWITCH   You've come to borrow money?

TARA   You should've said . . .

SWITCH   Is that right?

TARA   (*she carries on drinking in the surroundings*)
                Look. I know this is a bad time. I hate having
                to do this. It's just . . . I promised Nick I'd do
                the lunches. For the reading. I don't have
                anything.

                (*Beat.*)

SWITCH   Go to bed with me . . .

TARA   (*taken aback*) What?

SWITCH   I want you to go to bed with me.

TARA   Now?

                (*Beat.*)

SWITCH   Why not?

                (*Beat.*)

TARA   I have to be in Highbury. In about ten
                minutes . . .

SWITCH   Up to you.

TARA   Look. You know how important this is . . .

SWITCH   Whatever.

TARA   It might be the start of something.

SWITCH   Like what?

                (*Long pause. Each contemplates the other.*)

TARA   Look, forget it.

SWITCH   How much?

TARA   (*starting to go*) I said forget it.

                (*She goes off. Almost running. Off stage, a
                door slams.* SWITCH *remains motionless for a
                second. Then, suddenly convulsed with anger,
                he lashes out, sending a chair cartwheeling
                across the room. The chair connects with a
                rickety shelf/cupboard unit, which collapses
                in a heap onto the floor, bringing a cargo of
                breakables down with it. The noise and the
                mess are overwhelming.* SWITCH *sits on the
                edge of the bed. From below, someone bangs
                on the ceiling. A dog starts to bark. A
                terrible, unbearable bleakness. At length*
                SWITCH *rises, and, pausing briefly to weigh up
                what he is about to do, he pulls a mobile
                phone from his pocket and dials a number.*)

SWITCH   Andrew Bennett. Features. Just tell him a
                friend.

                (*Pause.*)

                (*downbeat*) Hi, Andy. Yeah . . . Listen. I
                might have something for you . . .

                (*Slow fade.*)

                        Scene Seven

A prison visiting room. Several months later.

RICHIE *sits across the table from* SWITCH.

RICHIE   I still don't understand. A full-page spread. In
                the *Sunday Times*. 'How this man steals your
                money.' And a big fuck-off photo – I mean,
                obviously of you – next to a sign reading DSS
                Harrow Road. What the fuck was going on in
                your head?

SWITCH	Don't look now . . .
RICHIE	What?
SWITCH	Next table but one.
RICHIE	Where?
SWITCH	Linford Christie's brother's killer. I said don't look now . . .
RICHIE	Switch . . .
SWITCH	You know what the police called the operation? Operation 'Fats'. I found out later. Who said the plods had no sense of humour?

(*Beat.*)

RICHIE	So what's it like?
SWITCH	Prison? Like grammar school but with fewer fuck-ups.
RICHIE	Seriously . . .
SWITCH	I'm in therapy. Did you know that? My lawyer reckons I've got a better chance of parole if I can prove I'm addressing my 'offending behaviour.'
RICHIE	Which is what?
SWITCH	That's what they're trying to work out. If they can cure the drugs habit, maybe I'll stop pretending to be other people, stealing their money. On the other hand, if they can sort out the impersonation thing – this not wanting to be me – maybe that'll cure the drug habit. Also the cigar habit, the Sainsbury's habit and the expensive holidays abroad habit.
RICHIE	What do you think?

SWITCH   Face it. I'm just a lazy sod. I want something
                for nothing and that's the end of it.

                (*Beat.*)

                It's funny. First Saturday I was here it was the
                Anniversary of The Funeral. We were all
                watching in the Rec. I said to this bloke – he's
                a nutter, but a religious one, so I should've
                known better – I said to him, imagine, Philip
                and the Queen Mother in the back with Di,
                that really *would've* been a result. He was
                shocked. Went round telling everyone what I'd
                said. So it comes up in Discussion. This thing
                we have, where we all sit around 'fessing up.
                And they're all agreed. I use comedy to hide
                'my inner hurt'. My inner hurt? Like anyone
                gives a fuck about some thick Sloane who
                bought dresses . . .

RICHIE   Perhaps they meant in general . . .

SWITCH   What?

RICHIE   I dunno. You turn everything into a joke. Or
                something . . .

SWITCH   Mum was laughing all the way to the Chapel.
                When she opened her Sunday paper . . .

                (*Pause.*)

RICHIE   You didn't mind me coming?

SWITCH   Why should I? To see one's friend run over is
                after all a unique and special pleasure . . .

RICHIE   What do you mean?

SWITCH   I feel like a prize exhibit in some Roman
                emperor's zoo. A captured Vandal chieftain.
                Or a camelopard. The Government has its

trophy. And my friends . . . my friends have something to come and gawp at . . .

RICHIE That's not fair.

SWITCH It's true, though. Isn't it?

(*Pause.* RICHIE is embarrassed.)

RICHIE Ever hear from Lisa?

SWITCH She was here. She's got a place at college. To do one of those teacher conversion things.

RICHIE Yeah?

SWITCH Just think. This time next year she'll be out in the world, filling the nation's children with unfulfillable expectations.

RICHIE How is she?

SWITCH Good. Better. Much better . . .

(*Pause.*)

RICHIE What about Tara. You ever speak to her?

SWITCH (*laughs*) Apparently she came into some money. (*Beat.*) You remember that playwright? The one she was about to shag? She set up this company with him. She puts on his plays, he spends her money. It's a perfect arrangement.

RICHIE Switch . . .

SWITCH What about you? I keep checking the club listings. In the *Weekend Guardian* . . .

RICHIE I kind of knocked the DJ-ing on the head. Just for a while. Thought I'd try my hand at something else.

SWITCH	Don't tell me. You're writing the screenplay.
RICHIE	What?
SWITCH	A moving tale for our times. Starring Ewan MacGregor and . . . somebody else.

(*Pause.*)

RICHIE	How did you know?
SWITCH	(*shrugs*) The Psychology of the Individual. As Jeeves would've put it.

(*Pause.*)

RICHIE	Are you angry?
SWITCH	About what?
RICHIE	About what happened?
SWITCH	Come to the group. See if you can work it out. (*Beat.*) Look. You didn't make this happen. (*Beat.*) I made this happen.
RICHIE	You wanted to be caught . . .
SWITCH	I don't know. Maybe . . .
RICHIE	But they never . . . you know . . .
SWITCH	They nailed me for Clark, Fisher and Jones. I held my hand up to three others. Chapman, Rees and Marshall. There's nothing to connect me, Stephen Waller, with the Mr Stephens who found that body – then vanished – or the Terry Newman who lived in that flat. Apparently.

(*Pause.* RICHIE *absorbs the details of* SWITCH'S *final act of legerdemain.*)

RICHIE	So what happens next?

SWITCH   Business as usual. I take drugs, I watch
              television, I organise the cockroach racing.

RICHIE   I meant after. After you get out.

              (*Beat.*)

SWITCH   It's funny. I've got quite friendly with my
              cellmate. Not the one I told you about – the
              one who nailed himself to the bunk – the new
              one, the one after. He's a car thief – though
              obviously not a particularly good one. Turns
              out he roadied for the Clash – did their first
              ever UK tour. Anyway we're talking one
              night, and he says to me, 'Face it, Prof' –
              that's what they call me. Professor. Pretty
              original, huh? – 'face it, if you ever met one
              of us on the outside, you'd walk right past on
              the other side of the road. Wouldn't you?' I
              felt like Alistair Sim. In one of those forties
              comedies. The clever toff with his hand caught
              in the till. And then I tried to explain. You
              know. How I didn't judge people by their –
              class, or what they *did* – but by something
              else. You know. Some sense of . . . *values* . . .
              of knowing what's bullshit and what isn't.
              Basically . . . whether they were . . . cool
              people or not. And he asked me what I meant
              by cool. Cool people. And I thought for a
              moment. And I tried to answer him. And then
              I realised I couldn't. I couldn't give him an
              answer. I had no fucking idea what I was
              talking about . . . .

RICHIE   I actually saw Lisa. I didn't tell you. She told
              me what she said. About this house.

SWITCH   Did she tell you about the money? How she got
              the money? (*Beat.*) This is the good bit.
              Apparently the last album just went platinum
              in Indonesia. It's part of the whole meltdown
              thing. All the kids stopped driving around in
              their parents Mercedes, started taking heroin

and listening to Blue Roses albums. It's like, welcome to the ruins, kids.

RICHIE   And?

SWITCH   And what?

RICHIE   Are you gonna go for it?

SWITCH   The deal is, keep my nose clean, stay out of trouble, the basement's mine.

RICHIE   That's what she told me.

             (*Beat.*)

SWITCH   When I walk out of here I'll be thirty-six years old. Think about it. I've had two days paid employment in my life. I'm just going to walk into some job, sort out my pension, start playing Sunday morning football with Tony and Darren from Marketing? How the fuck am I gonna stay out of trouble? (*Beat.*) 'Come in Mr Waller. Sit down Mr Waller. We were intrigued by this eleven year gap in your CV . . . '

RICHIE   It's what she wants.

             (*A voice booms from offstage.*)

WARDER   That's time, gentlemen.

             (*Beat.*)

SWITCH   I have to go.

RICHIE   Think about it.

SWITCH   I will.

             (*He gets up. Prepares to say good-bye. Then checks. A sudden thought.*)

How does it end?

RICHIE   What?

SWITCH   The screenplay. Don't tell me he gets the
                  girl . . .

                  (*If* RICHIE *knows the answer to this, then he is
                  giving nothing away.*)

                  Whatever. Send me a copy when it's finished.

                  (*He starts to go.*)

                  I'd like to read it . . .

                  (*Fade to black.*)

                  THE END